YOUNG EXPLORERS
NATURE JOURNAL

Observing Activities

for Exploring Nature Outdoors

BY NATURALIST

STEPHEN NETT

COVER ILLUSTRATION

RY MENSON

Brightling Publishing
brightlingpublish@stephennettkids.com

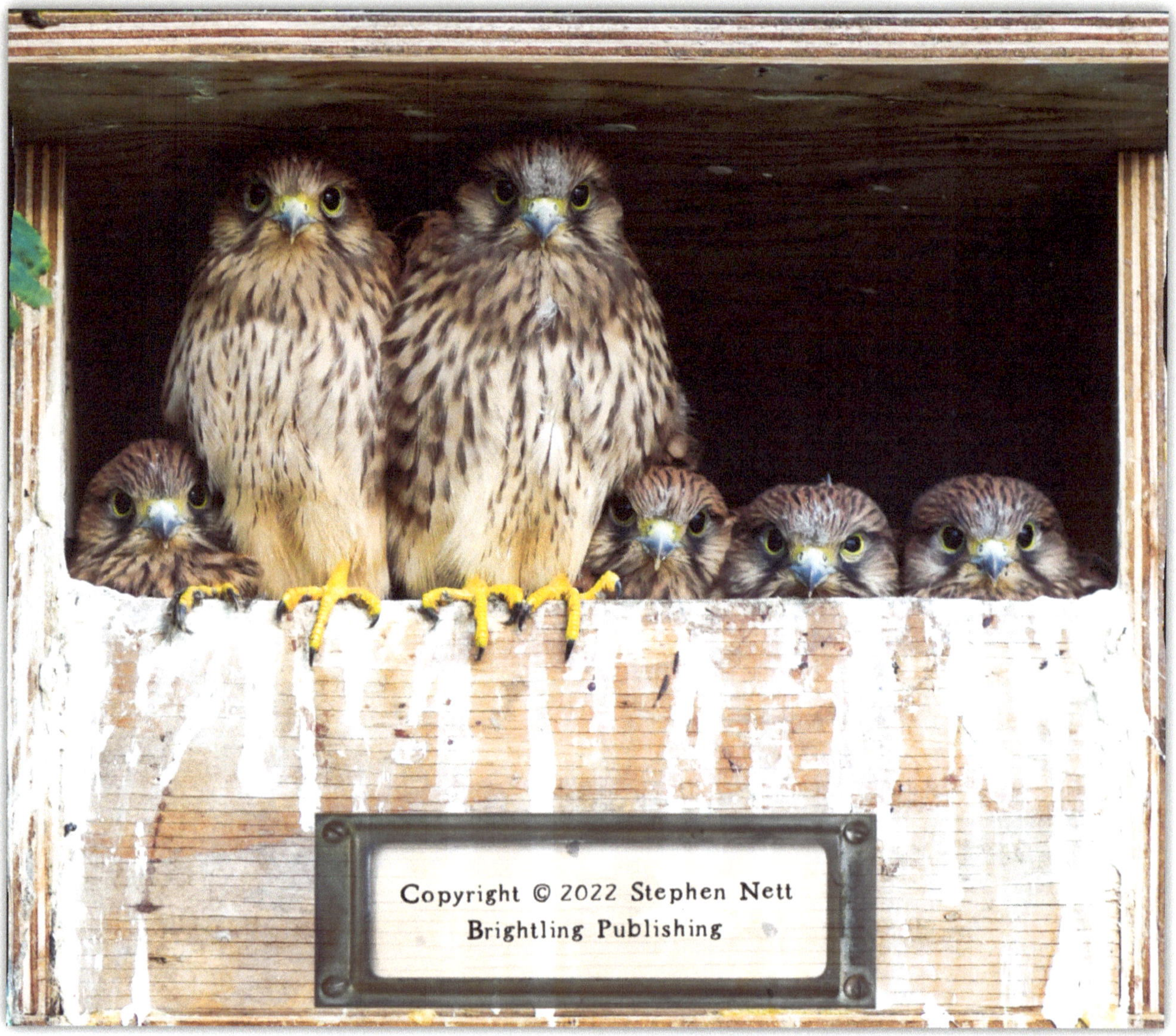

To Rowan, Theo and Atlas
- Wonder Well -

And To the Brood Who've Flown the Nest
Tasha, Jason, Nicole and Marissa

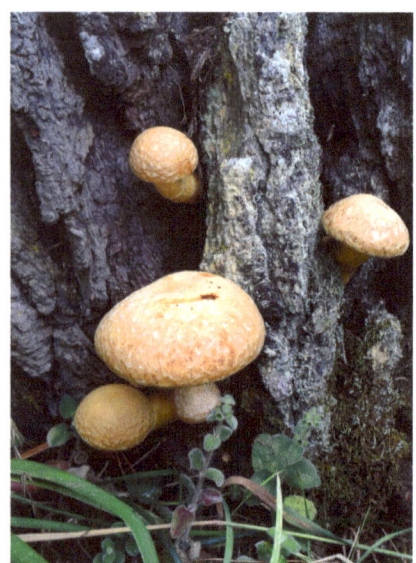

For Journal refills, additional copies, tips or questions
Contact: snettkids@stephennettkids.com

Choose safety first. Since we can't be there, the author and publisher must disclaim any liability in connection with use of this information.

ISBN: 979-8-9861065-0-2
Library of Congress Control Number pending.

BRIGHTLING

At Brightling Publishing we focus on books and materials that help strengthen personal connection with the natural world. We believe those connections are the essential key to our mutual future, and to the type of world we leave future generations. We think children should be given the chance to love nature before they're asked to save it.

Brightling Publishing LLC Bodega Bay California

Find More Nature, Hike and Camp Ideas at www.stephennettkids.com

This Journal Belongs to

_____

AN
EXPLORER

MY MISSION IS TO HAVE FUN DISCOVERING THE WORLD I LIVE IN

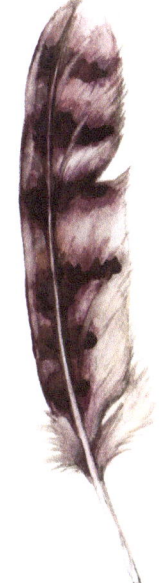

PARENTS & TEACHERS - SEE GUIDES on PAGE 50-51

NATURE AND ME

Yes you!

I HAVE ABILITIES INSIDE ME FOR EXPLORING, DISCOVERING, AND HAVING FUN IN NATURE.

MY abilities will help me discover hidden secrets and wonders in nature.

MY abilities will grow stronger when I spend time exploring nature outside.

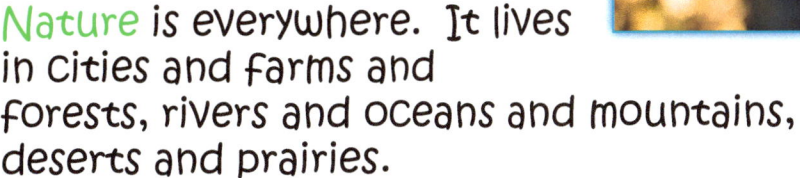

I can explore nature in my yard, on my street, in parks and fields and wild places.

Nature is everywhere. It lives in cities and farms and forests, rivers and oceans and mountains, deserts and prairies.

I am part of nature, too. And that's why I have special abilities for exploring nature.

Amazing Exploring Abilities

SOME ABILITIES WE HAVE:

CURIOSITY – makes you wonder and want to ask questions about new things. Like, What is this? Where does this path go? What will I discover next?

SIGHT - for noticing things like colors, movement, light and dark (like shadows), shapes and patterns.

HEARING – to catch sounds nearby and far away, tiny soft or roaring loud, high whistles and low rumbles, noises made by all kinds of things.

SMELL – sweet or stinky, strong or barely there. With practice our noses can even smell hiding animals, places with water, and more flowers and plants.

FEELING – our skin can feel sunlight, wind, and things that touch us. Our skin can tell us if things are soft or hard or smooth or cold or wet. Our bodies can feel when we are moving, slipping, climbing or falling.

EMOTIONS - we can feel excited or surprised, happy or sad, nervous or peaceful, scared or safe, caring and loving. These feelings can help guide us in nature too.

MEMORY – we have the ability to remember all the things we find and observe in nature - and where to find them again, and what their names are too.

IMAGINATION - helps us wonder about the things we discover, make up stories and games about them, and get ideas about what they are and how they work.

WRITING AND DRAWING – our ability to create pictures, names, notes and stories helps us save our discoveries and share them with other people.

WHAT OTHER ABILITIES DO YOU HAVE?

LET'S OBSERVE!

Our most important skill is – OBSERVING.

OBSERVING is using all of your sensing abilities to notice things around you.

Observing is noticing movement, color, sound, smell, shapes and patterns, hot and cold, smooth and rough...

... cute or strange or amazing things. Big things, little things, hidden things. Anything that makes you curious.

We're observing when we feel raindrops on our skin. That can tell us what's happening with the weather.

We're observing when we see movement, and find a rabbit watching us.

We're observing when we hear chirping in one tree, and then the same chirping from a different tree.

It's two birds talking to each other!

To observe BEST, use more than one Ability

Here's an example.

If we discover some flowers

First, we may notice a flower's color with our **eyes**,

then **feel** the smooth petals with our fingers,

and then we may be curious about how it **smells**.

If we observe the flower for a little while, we may discover creatures visiting it.

Observe how they move – do they fly or crawl or hop?

What do you think they're doing?

Now look around - are there other kinds of flowers and creatures nearby?

WE are GREAT Observers!

Once, all fathers, mothers and children had to use their observing abilities outside to find food and water and homes, not get lost, and to get along with all the other creatures who live in Nature.

THAT'S WHY YOU HAVE SO MANY SENSING ABILITIES.

Wild animals are really Great Observers too!

They may be observing YOU.

If you get too close, they may fly or run away or hide, or make noises to warn other creatures.

THERE ARE MANY WAYS TO OBSERVE NATURE — IT'S FUN TO FIND THE WAYS YOU LIKE BEST, AND PRACTICE TO BECOME AN EXPERT OBSERVER.

HOW TO USE YOUR JOURNAL

1 Explore — Walk outside and discover places in nature

2 Find — Find interesting and wonderful things

3 Observe — Use your sensing abilities to discover more about them

4 Journal — Draw, color, write and save your discoveries in your Explorers Journal

5 Repeat — Observe again another time. Find what changes! You'll get better and better!

Look for me, the Bluebird. I'll show you fun things to try!

CIRCLE

The WEATHER is

WRITE

Today is

_____

DRAW
COLOR
WRITE
TAPE
TRACE

here

My Story

GO EXPLORE!
Let's practice Observing

Come Outside and Discover!!

LOOK AROUND AND FIND A TREE YOU LIKE.

 Listen - is the tree making any sounds? The branches may creak or the leaves may shush if there's a breeze or wind.

Is there movement or sound in the tree from creatures, like bees or birds or squirrels?

 What color or pattern are they wearing?

 Are things growing on the tree, like moss or vines or ferns?

 Does the bark have a smell?

 Feel the bark - is it smooth or rough?

 Check on the ground around the tree - are there any mushrooms or insects?

GREAT OBSERVING

Nature is filled with secrets – but they'll stay hidden til you observe them. Here are some ways to go observing and exploring.

Sometimes we can observe more by moving!

Walk and Spy

WALK SOMEWHERE YOU'VE NEVER BEEN BEFORE.

Observe UP above you, DOWN on the ground, UNDER things and BEHIND things. You never know what you'll find.

When you're walking, watch for movement all around you.

Birds, insects and other animals may be using their senses and observe *you* coming. You may cause slither them to fly, hop, or away.

If you see where they went, you can try to get closer.

Don't forget to listen too: birds and animals often make calls or sounds when they observe us. They may be saying:

LOOK OUT ~ HUMAN COMING!

Sometimes we observe more by being still!

MORE OBSERVING

Sit and Scan 1

FIND AN INTERESTING PLACE TO SIT DOWN.

 Use your hands like pretend binoculars - look through the circles formed by your fingers.

 Look close by, far away, up in the trees or sky, or anywhere.

What do you see when you look?

 See if you can spot:

Flowers Berries Trees Leaves Birds
Lizards Beetles Bees

Sit and Scan 2

 Now use your pretend binoculars to look down at the ground around you.

 What is the tiniest plant you can find? Do you see any really little creatures?

 Do you see any interesting or pretty rocks or sticks? Try looking under some and see what you can discover.

Sometimes if we look very closely, we can find entire little worlds around us.

FIND NATURE'S TREASURES

Let's Go Find some!

Treasure Hunt

FLOWERS AND LEAVES HUNT

FLOWERS AND LEAVES COME IN MANY MANY DIFFERENT SHAPES AND COLORS AND SIZES AND PATTERNS AND SMELLS

 How many different kinds of FLOWERS can you find? Draw, trace or take pictures.

 How many shapes of LEAVES can you find? Trace, draw or tape inside your Journal.

Hear Near and Far

NATURE SOUNDS

 Close your eyes and listen – what can you hear?

 Are the sounds near or far away?

 Are the sounds moving?

 What could be making those sounds?

Where's Water?

EVERY LIVING THING NEEDS WATER TO DRINK.
SO FINDING WATER IS REALLY IMPORTANT.

 Water falls from clouds.
Can you find where it goes?

 Can you find drops  of water?

 Can you find puddles or ponds of water?

 Can you find any streams or creeks with water in them? Stay safe!

Where else could water be?

Animal Snack Bar

MANY PLANTS MAKE BERRIES, FRUITS, SEEDS, NUTS OR ACORNS, WHICH ANIMALS EAT AS FOOD.

A GREAT WAY TO DISCOVER ANIMALS IS TO WATCH FOODS THEY LIKE TO EAT.
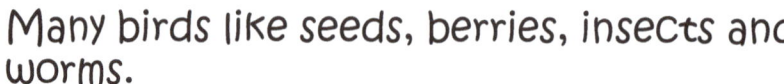

Watch flowers for hummingbirds, bees and butterflies.

Squirrels and chipmunks love acorns and nuts.

Many birds like seeds, berries, insects and worms.

Rabbits, mice and gophers like leaves and grass.

Some animals, like hawks and snakes, hunt other animals.

Filling Your NATURE JOURNAL

Use your Journal to hold your discoveries!!

This Exploring Nature Journal will help you collect and share the interesting things you discover while exploring.

Use your Journal to

make drawings and pictures

give things names

collect leaves and flowers and photos

write stories and notes and poems and songs

Things You Can Do

 Draw and color the things you observe.
Colored pencils and crayons work best.

 Trace around a leaf or flower, to copy it's shape.

 Tape favorite leaves or flowers in your Journal.

 Make up a story about the creatures you see.
What do you think they were doing?

 Give special names to things you discover,
or learn the names other explorers gave them.

 Use your imagination and curiosity to make up a game.

Watch for these Special Things

Can you find these outside?

These Seven Things are really super especially important in Nature.

Observing them is the best way to discover nature's wonders.

1 **Land**

Was I UP HIGH or DOWN LOW?

What is the GROUND like?

- Desert
- Valley
- Hill
- Mountain
- Rocks
- Sand
- Grass
- Dirt

2 **Water**

What WATER did I find?

- Drops
- Puddle
- Pond
- Ocean
- Creek
- River
- Lake

3 **Flowers**

What different kinds of FLOWERS did I find?

4 **Leaves**

What different kinds of LEAVES did I find?

What SHAPES and COLORS and SMELLS did you observe?

 **Trees**

Do the TREES you see have Different....

- Shapes
- Bark
- Leaves
- Size

 **Seeds and Fruit**

How Do they Travel?

- Wind Sailing
- Grabby or Sticky
- Popping Pods
- Eaten by Animals
- Fall and Roll
- Float on Water

 **Animals**

Sometimes it's hard to find animals. But

 **Can you find SIGNS where animals have been ....**

Walking   Eating   Pooping   Nesting

Why are these 7 so Special?

These things make Nature work.

 **1** **Land**

The shape of the LAND, from mountains to valleys to flat plains, creates different kinds of habitats for creatures to live in.

 **2** **Water**

The amount of WATER changes what kinds of life - fish, amphibians, insects, animals and plants - can live there.

 **3** **Flowers**

FLOWERS make food for bees, butterflies and many other creatures, and help plants make new plants.

 **4** **Leaves**

LEAVES use starlight (from our Sun) to make things like sugar and wood, the oxygen we breathe, and things for many creatures to eat.

 **5** **Trees**

TREES are homes for many kinds of creatures, and also create forests that are habitats for many more.

 **6** **Seeds and Fruit**

SEEDS and FRUIT not only feed many creatures, they also help plants spread to new places.

 **7** **Animals**

ANIMALS often live in groups and communities that help maintain the habitats of other creatures.

Be Safe

Ooops.

What to Bring ....

Something to drink, clothes to get dirty in, a hat and jacket in case it gets cold or rainy, a snack, a whistle, your Journal, color pencils or crayons. Have a special carrying bag or small pack just for your adventures.

Don't taste or eat things you find unless an adult says it's safe. Some things that are good for animals can be bad news for humans.

Moving water, like creeks, rivers and the ocean, can have a strong pull. Ask an adult before going into any water.

You can use a safe bug spray to keep mosquitoes and ticks away. Check your clothes for ticks after hiking.

Most animals are afraid of us and will try to stay away if they can. Some snakes and spiders may be surprised if you uncover their hiding place - so be careful where you put your hands and feet.

Wild animals don't like to be touched. Try not to scare them, which might make them scratch, bite or sting to protect themselves.

Stay Together. Carry your own loud whistle.

If you get Lost....
find a big tree, make a nest, blow your whistle - toot, toot, toot - three times in a row, over and over. That's the "help me" signal. Then let adults come find you.

Plants like Poison Ivy, Sumac and Poison Oak can make us scratch and itch! Watch for them and don't touch or rub against them.

THE BEST WAY TO BE SAFE IN NATURE IS TO LEARN AS MUCH AS YOU CAN ABOUT NATURE

Today is _____

Where am I _____

The WEATHER is

 # My Discoveries

Land I Discovered

Water I Discovered

Draw some Flower SHAPES and COLORS

Flowers I Discovered

Animals

Animals I SAW

Animals I HEARD

Seeds and Fruit and BERRIES and NUTS I Discovered

Trees   I Discovered

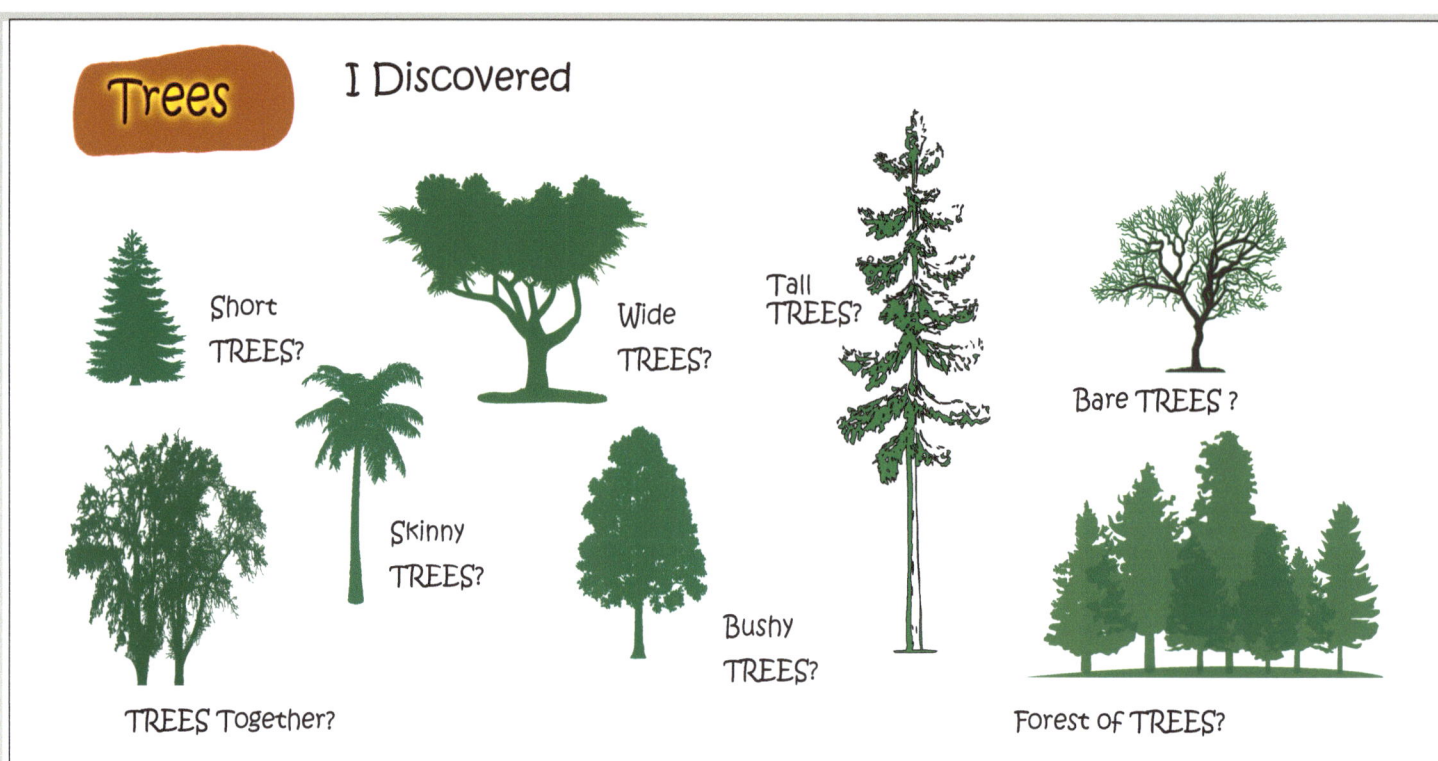

Short TREES?

Skinny TREES?

Wide TREES?

Bushy TREES?

Tall TREES?

Bare TREES?

TREES Together?

Forest of TREES?

Leaves   I Discovered

Trace, Draw, Color or Tape some LEAVES here:

Draw or Write Stories or Discoveries Here

Today is _____

Where am I _____

The WEATHER is

 # My Discoveries

Land   I Discovered

Water   I Discovered

Draw some Flower SHAPES and COLORS

Flowers   I Discovered

Animals

Animals I SAW

Animals I HEARD

Seeds and Fruit and BERRIES and NUTS I Discovered

Trees

I Discovered

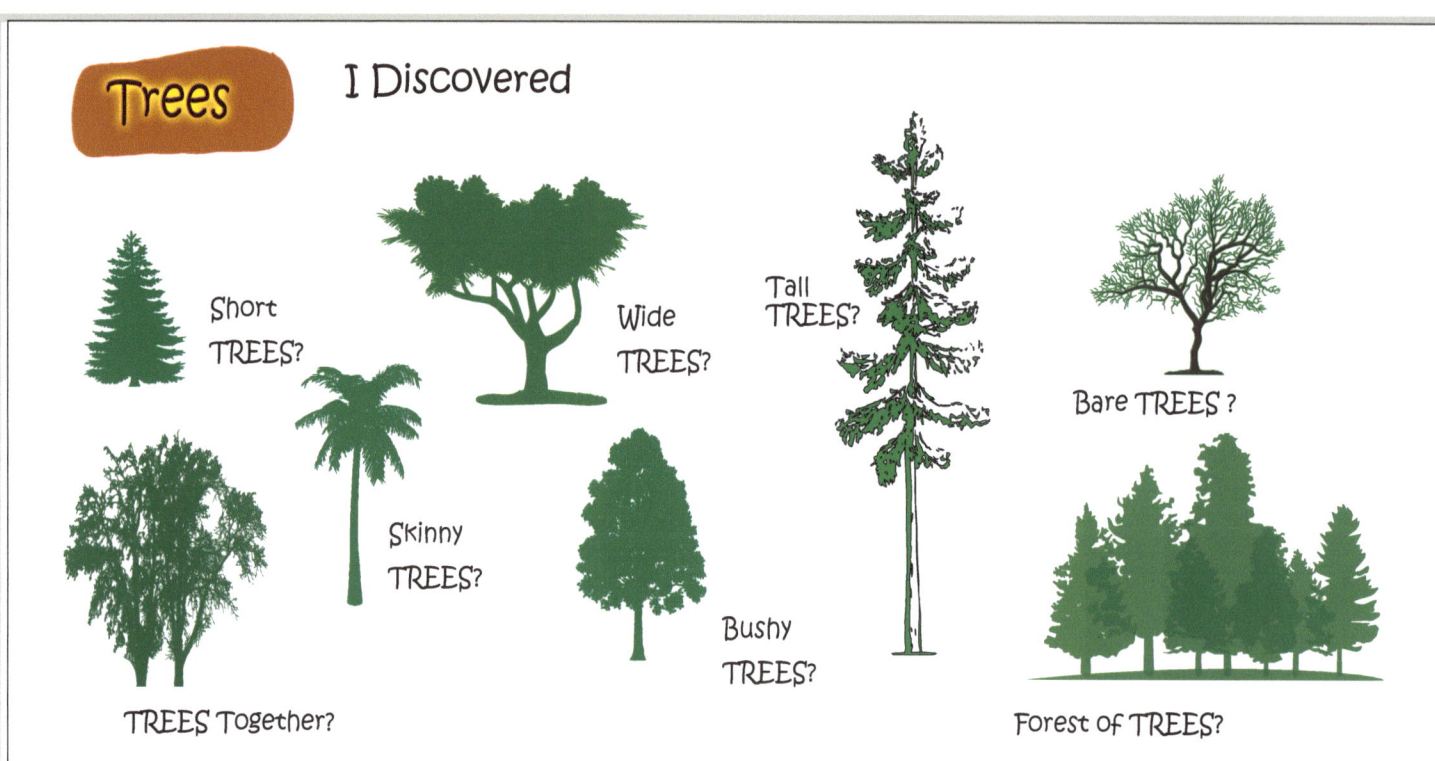

Short TREES?

Wide TREES?

Tall TREES?

Bare TREES?

Skinny TREES?

Bushy TREES?

TREES Together?

Forest of TREES?

Leaves

I Discovered

Trace, Draw, Color or Tape some LEAVES here:

Draw or Write Stories or Discoveries Here

Today is _____

Where am I _____

The WEATHER is

 # My Discoveries

Land   I Discovered

Water   I Discovered

Draw some Flower SHAPES and COLORS

Flowers   I Discovered

Animals

Animals I SAW

Animals I HEARD

Seeds and Fruit
and BERRIES and NUTS I Discovered

Trees   I Discovered

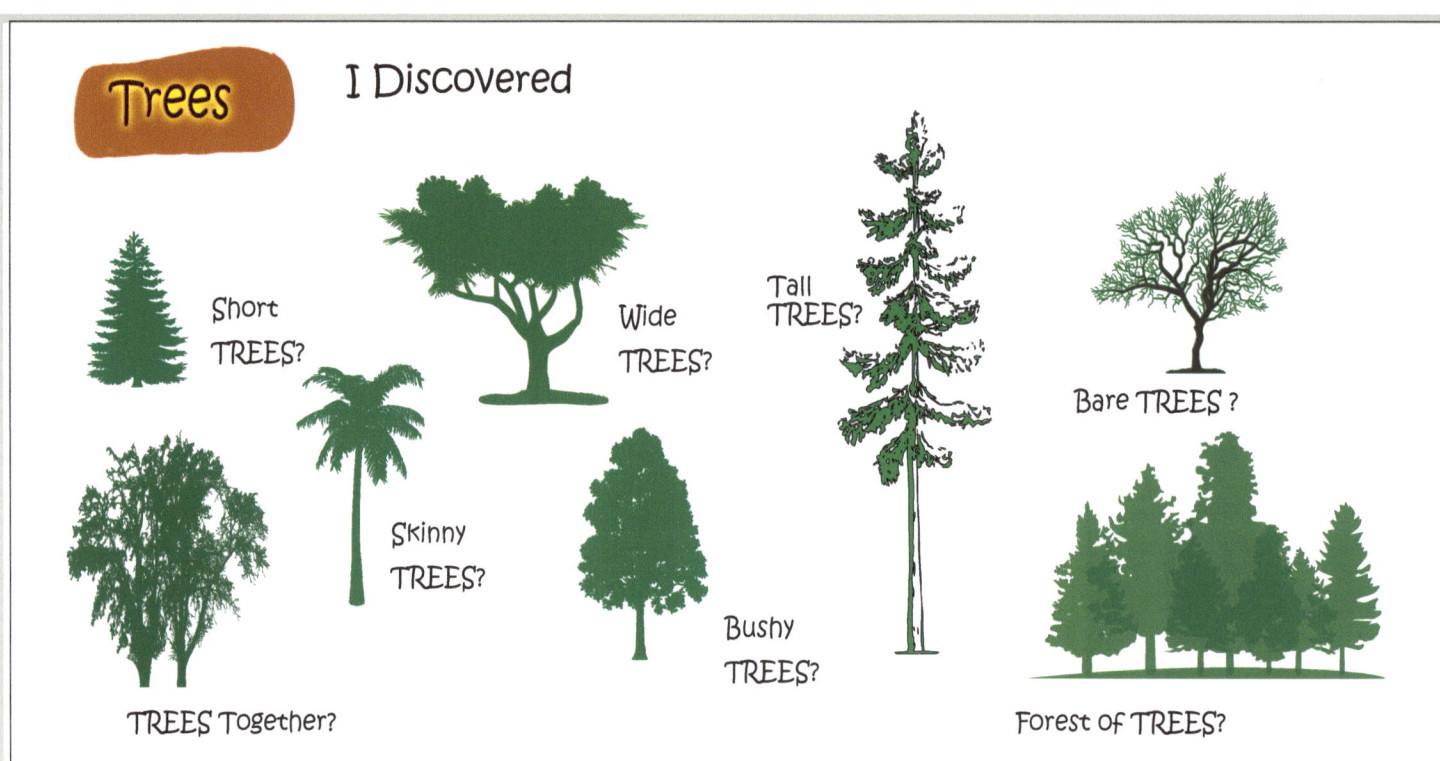

Short TREES?

Wide TREES?

Tall TREES?

Bare TREES?

Skinny TREES?

Bushy TREES?

TREES Together?

Forest of TREES?

Leaves   I Discovered

Trace, Draw, Color or Tape some LEAVES here:

Draw or Write Stories or Discoveries Here

Today is _____

Where am I _____

The WEATHER is

 # My Discoveries

Land   I Discovered

Water   I Discovered

Draw some Flower SHAPES and COLORS

Flowers   I Discovered

34

Animals

Animals I SAW

Animals I HEARD

Seeds and Fruit and BERRIES and NUTS I Discovered

Trees

I Discovered

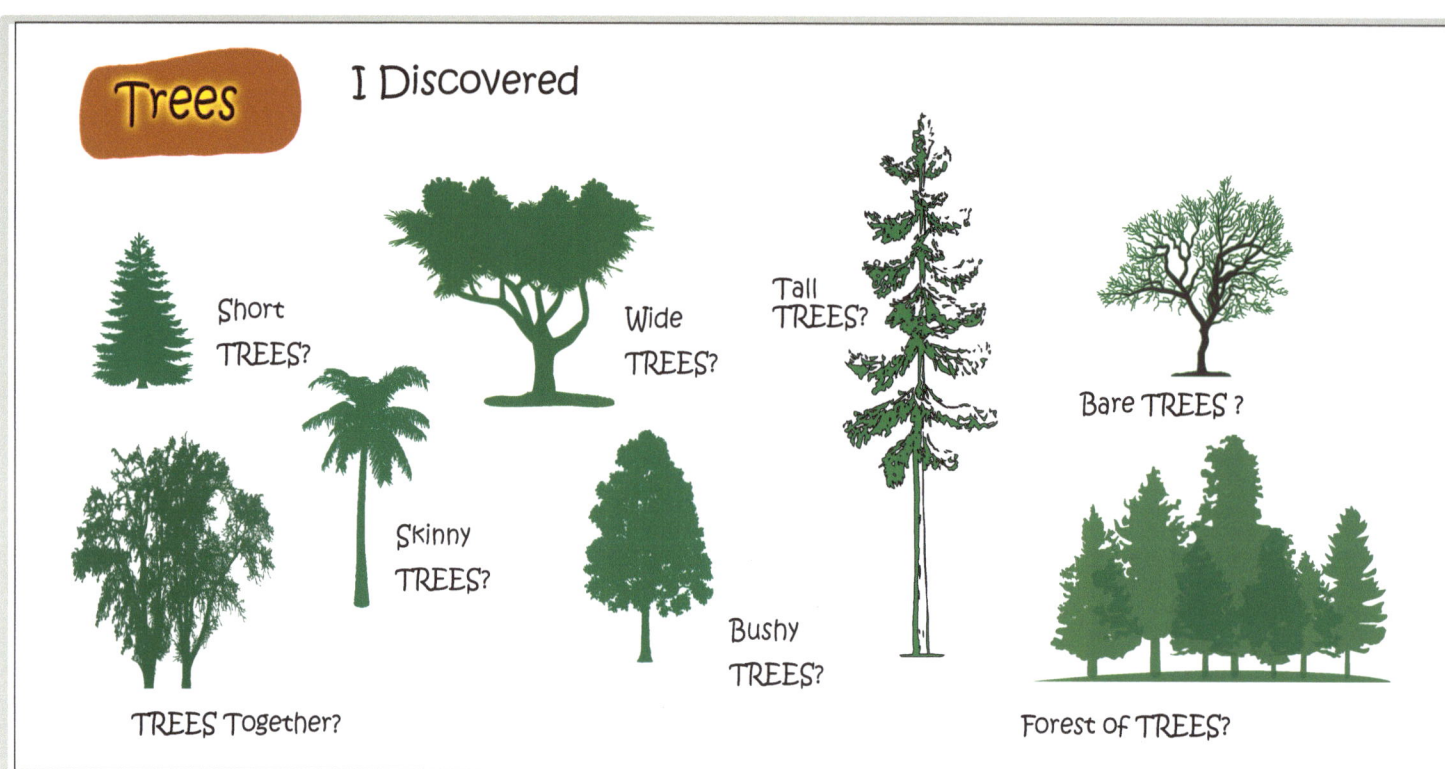

Short TREES?

Wide TREES?

Tall TREES?

Bare TREES ?

Skinny TREES?

Bushy TREES?

TREES Together?

Forest of TREES?

Leaves

I Discovered

Trace, Draw, Color or Tape some LEAVES here:

Today is _____

Where am I _____

The WEATHER is

My Discoveries

 Land I Discovered

 Water I Discovered

Draw some Flower SHAPES and COLORS

Flowers I Discovered

38

Animals

Animals I SAW

Animals I HEARD

Seeds and Fruit and BERRIES and NUTS I Discovered

Trees

I Discovered

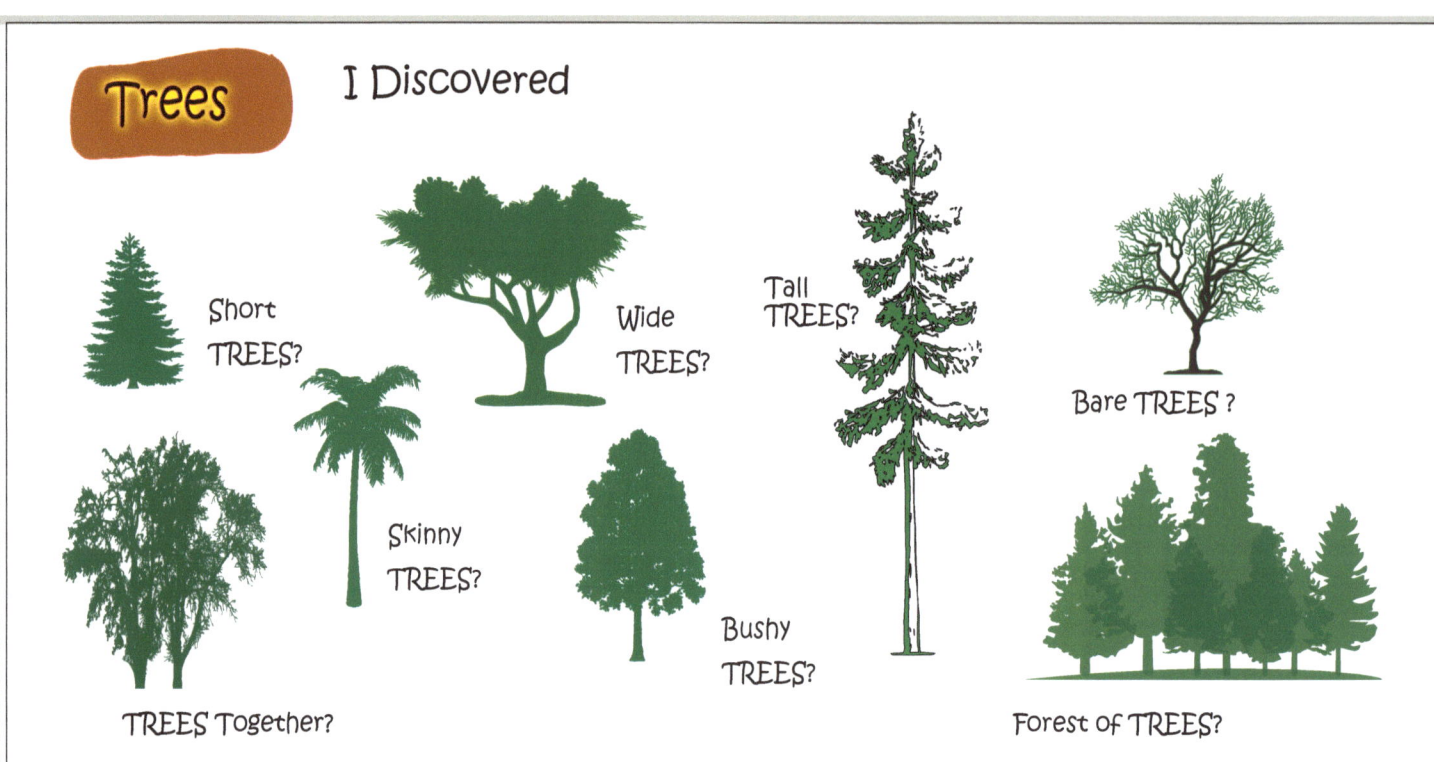

Short TREES?

Wide TREES?

Skinny TREES?

Tall TREES?

Bare TREES?

Bushy TREES?

TREES Together?

Forest of TREES?

Leaves

I Discovered

Trace, Draw, Color or Tape some LEAVES here:

Draw or Write Stories or Discoveries Here

Today is _____

Where am I _____

The WEATHER is

 # My Discoveries

Land   I Discovered

Water   I Discovered

Draw some Flower SHAPES and COLORS

Flowers   I Discovered

42

Animals

Animals I SAW

Animals I HEARD

Seeds and Fruit and BERRIES and NUTS I Discovered

Trees

I Discovered

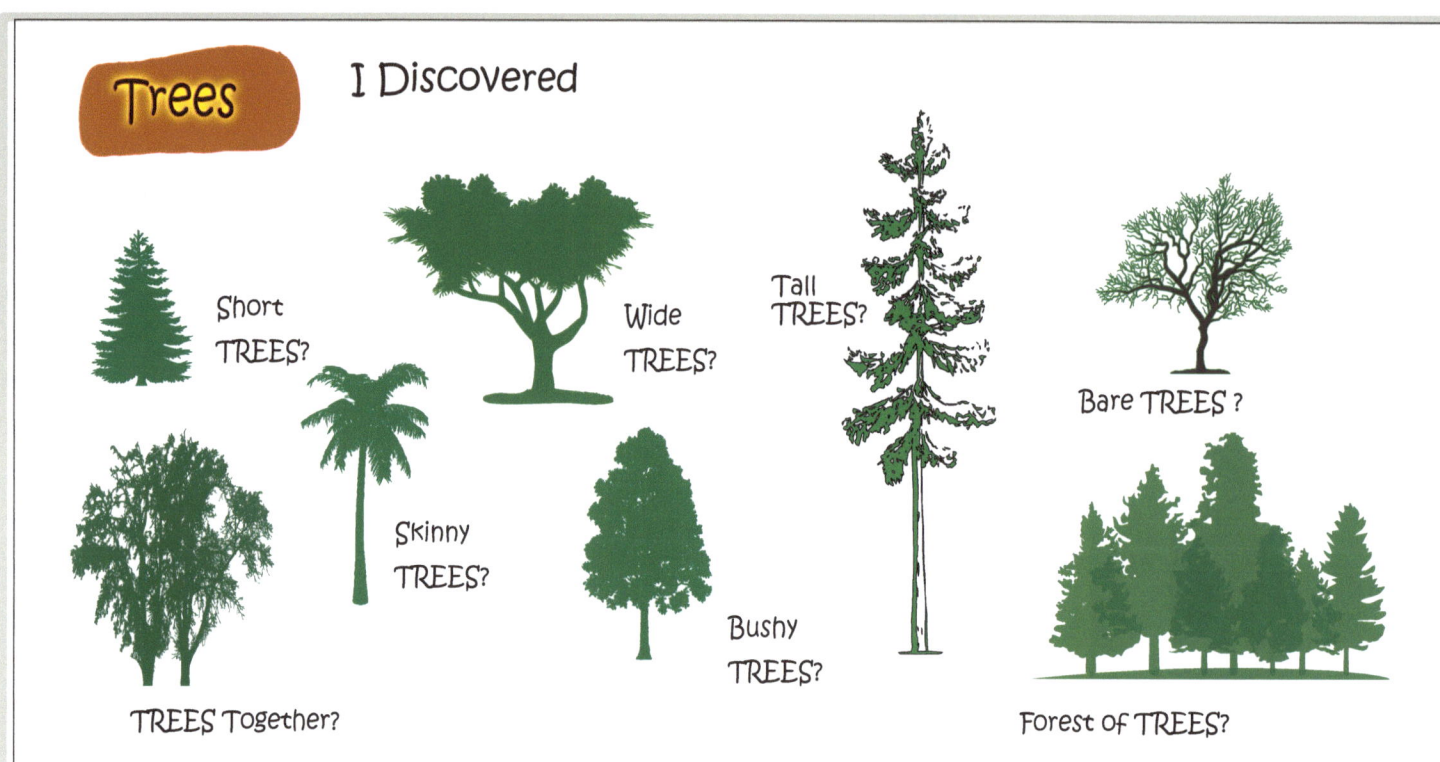

Short TREES?

Wide TREES?

Tall TREES?

Bare TREES ?

Skinny TREES?

Bushy TREES?

TREES Together?

Forest of TREES?

Leaves

I Discovered

Trace, Draw, Color or Tape some LEAVES here:

Today is _____

Where am I _____

The WEATHER is

My Discoveries

 **Land**   I Discovered

 **Water**   I Discovered

Draw some Flower SHAPES and COLORS

Flowers   I Discovered

Animals

Animals I SAW

Animals I HEARD

Seeds and Fruit and BERRIES and NUTS I Discovered

Trees

I Discovered

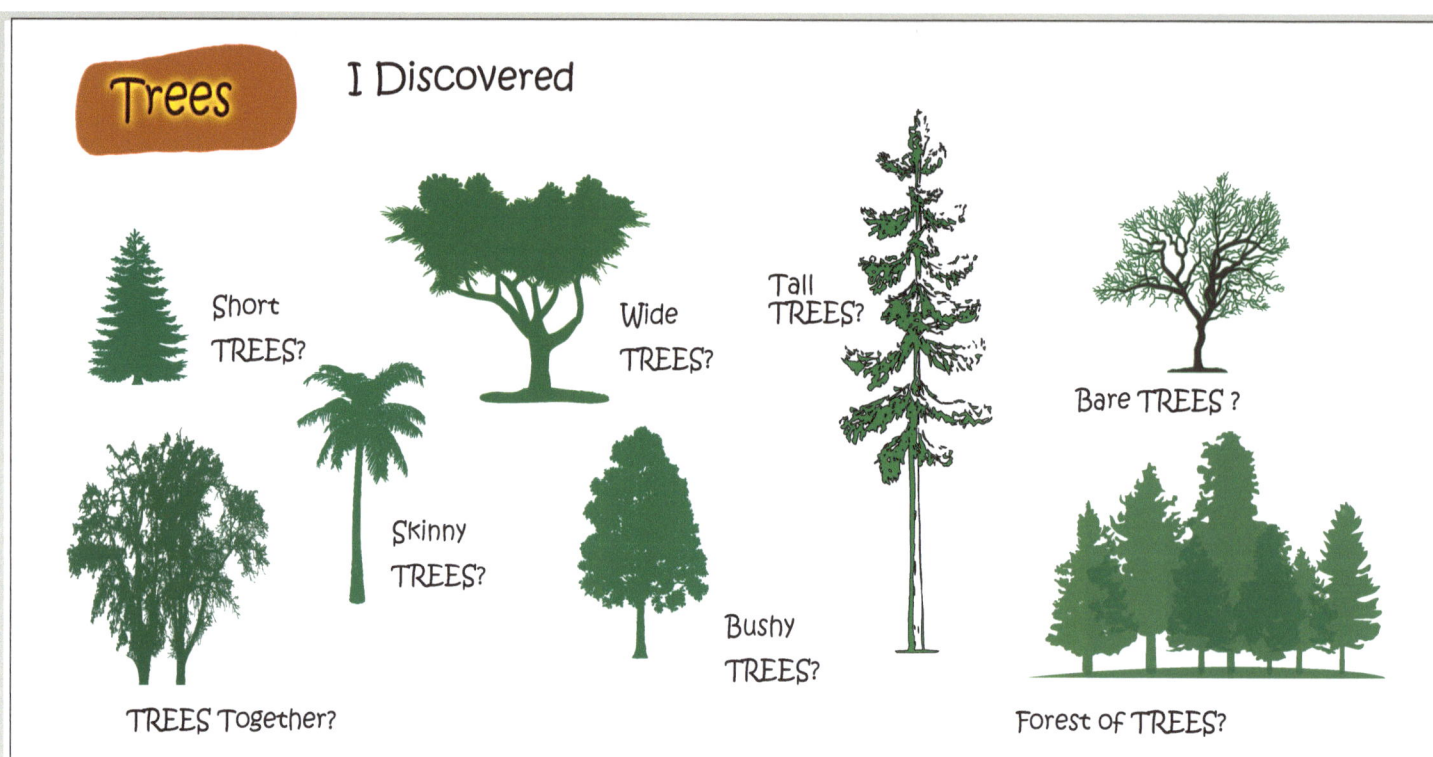

Short TREES?

Skinny TREES?

Wide TREES?

Bushy TREES?

Tall TREES?

Bare TREES?

TREES Together?

Forest of TREES?

Leaves

I Discovered

Trace, Draw, Color or Tape some LEAVES here:

FOR PARENTS AND TEACHERS

About this Journal

Before we had schools, children discovered the wonders of nature at the source, by exploring outdoors. With guidance, they learned how to read nature, find water and food, and make their way home again.

Things have changed. But fortunately, every child still comes fully loaded with the same sensory toolkit and inspiration for discovering nature. Kids happily use their exploring abilities, given a chance and a bit of help.

But where do we start?

As a Naturalist, I designed this Journal as an easy guide to help children discover their abilities, and nature's secrets. With simple tips to help build observing skills, easy to achieve activities, and lots of spaces to record what they find.

Most kids find this spontaneously good fun. It's their personal Journal of being in nature.

The observing activities focus on seven features: Land, Water, Flowers, Leaves, Seeds & Berries, Trees, and Animals. Easy to observe by even the youngest explorers, nearly everywhere. These 7 also form the essential framework of the natural world - which is why humans have always had to understand them to be safe and thrive.

The goal of this Journal is to help children use the sensory abilities they were born with, as they were intended: in nature.

There is no better, proven way to do that than to go outside, exploring. No class or video or app can match a discovery walk in a bird-filled park, or a prairie field, into a living forest, or along a shoreline at sunset.

Fortunately, many of nature's mysteries and wonders are just outside, and will reveal themselves with even a little attention. Endless more secrets are there to be uncovered once we know where and how to observe.

But the most important ingredient to discovering nature? It's you.

To children, the outdoors is a vast secret garden filled with surprises. And we hold the key to the gate.

Nothing can be more reassuring to children today than to discover for themselves that outdoors all around them, babies are being born and hatched, waves crash and stars sparkle, leaves grow, flowers open, berries ripen, trees soar, rivers run, winds blow, the sun rises, birds sing...

Would you take a moment to leave a review about this Journal?

And for more Nature Resources, Guides and Tips, visit us at

WWW.STEPHENNETTKIDS.COM

TIPS for ADULTS on USING THIS JOURNAL

For the best time in nature, have small goals to accomplish (like the ones in this Journal) - simple activities that focus our attention and let us get lost in the moment.

Children can have very different abilities, interests and comfort levels outdoors. It's important to let kids find their own and then grow from there. Encourage, entice, lead - don't push.

By using the same observing activities over and over we become a better and better observer. It's amazing what we miss the first or second time. Practice at different locations, but also at the same locations at different times of year. Discover what changes!

The Journal spaces can be filled in or left empty. Their real purpose is to strengthen observing skills by encouraging creative 'collecting'.

This Journal doesn't teach journaling - resources are available on our website and elsewhere. The focus here is on observing, because that is the first essential step to exploring and journaling and enjoyment.

Questions are a child's best tool for discovering nature. It isn't necessary to answer them immediately - wonder right along with them! *Looking for answers* is observing. Look up answers together, later.

Nature is filled with mysteries. Help children find them, and try to solve them. Ask "what do you think?" Let them use their imagination, hunt down clues. Surprises are their own reward!

It's ok for younger children to make up their own names for things if they want. Let the willow be the Grandmother tree, the worm be Wiggly, the hawk be Stormy. Names are for memories, and sharing.

If asked, share the names other explorers have assigned, (from Naturalist Guides and apps) to identify plants, animals, rocks, etc. But the goal of this Journal is to foster discovery, observation, wonder, connections, before scholarship.

For safety, have an outdoor plan that allows free exploration, but with agreed-on boundaries. Supervise from a distance that is safe for your child, your child's age and the place and time they're exploring.

Children may have concerns or even be afraid about the outdoors, especially if they don't have a lot of previous experience. Help them feel safe. Acknowledge concerns – don't brush them off - but teach respect for, not fear of, things that can harm us.

And remember, its good observing that keeps us safe!

PHOTO CREDITS

Joshua Gresham	Janice Gill	Ryan Stone
Abigail Keenan	Joshua J Cotten	Scott Walsh
Juliane Liebermann	Janko Ferlic	Yulia Dubyna
Alexander Dummer	Katherine Hanlon	Sean Duan
Caroline Hernandez	Sandy Milar	Zach Lucero
Cole Keister	Ryan Stone	Helena Lopes
Markus Spiske	Marcus Wallis	Frank Cone
Chris Lawton	Matteo Grando	Maddie Franz
Dorothea Oldani	Max Gohme	Mark Broadhurst
Eddie Black	Onder Ortel	Thijs Schouten
Emily Karakis	Mi Pham	Ricardo Esquivel
Evie Shaffer	Pete Nuij	Skyler Ewing
Felix Besombes	Photoholgic	Stephen Nett
Hulki Okan Tabak	Richard Sagredo	

Content, design and graphics by Stephen Nett

Special thanks to Andrea my wife
for inspiration, long hikes and patience

Natasha for joyful child expertise

And Bertha, who lit the spark